# Christmas Fever

ALSO BY NGOZI OLIVIA OSUOHA

*The Transformation Train*
*Letter to My Unborn*
*Sensation*
*Tropical Escape (with Amos O. Ojwang')*
*Fruits from the Poetry Planet*
*Poetic Grenade*
*Whispers of the Biafran Skeleton*
*Chains*
*Raindrops*
*Freeborn*
*Eclipse of Tides*
*The Subterfuge*
*Green Snake on a Green Grass*
*Chariots of Archangels*
*Wonderment*
*Interwoven*
*xenophobicracy*
*Destiny*
*The Phenomenal Human*

# Christmas Fever

poems by
**Ngozi Olivia Osuoha**

Poetic Justice Books
Port St. Lucie, Florida

©2020 Ngozi Olivia Osuoha

book design and layout: SpiNDec, Port Saint Lucie, FL
cover image: Zenith Bank Christmas Display, Lagos, Nigeria
cover design: Kris Haggblom

All rights reserved.

No part of this book may be used or reproduced in any manner whatsoever without written permission except in the case of brief quotations embodied in critical articles and reviews. Members of educational institutions and organizations wishing to photocopy any of the work for classroom use, or authors, artists and publishers who would like to obtain permission for any material in the work, should contact the publisher.

Published by Poetic Justice Books
Port Saint Lucie, Florida
www.poeticjusticebooks.com

ISBN: 978-1-950433-50-6

FIRST EDITION
10 9 8 7 6 5 4 3 2 1

*This book is dedicated to all those who died, got wounded, contracted strange sickness, or who were unfortunate in any form because they wanted to celebrate the birth of Jesus.*

## contents

| | |
|---|---:|
| JINGLES | 3 |
| WEATHER AND ATMOSPHERE | 4 |
| SEASON'S GREETINGS | 5 |
| NEW PRODUCTS | 6 |
| RITUALS | 7 |
| PROSTITUTION | 8 |
| STEALING | 9 |
| LIES | 10 |
| BUSINESS | 11 |
| PRICES OF GOODS | 12 |
| TRAVEL ARRANGEMENTS | 13 |
| PREPARATIONS | 14 |
| PRAYERS AND CRUSADES | 15 |
| DUPING | 16 |
| KIDNAPPING | 17 |
| CRIMES | 18 |
| MOVEMENTS | 19 |
| CONGESTIONS | 20 |
| LAND SPECULATIONS | 21 |
| SUITORS AND ARRANGEMENTS | 22 |
| MARRIAGES | 23 |
| MEETINGS | 24 |
| ABROAD GUYS | 25 |
| VILLAGE PEOPLE | 26 |
| PRIDE SHOWS | 27 |
| BURIALS | 28 |
| FOOTBALL COMPETITIONS | 29 |
| CEREMONIES | 30 |
| SIGHTSEEING | 31 |
| REUNIONS | 32 |

| | |
|---|---|
| MEMORIALS | 33 |
| GIFTS | 34 |
| LATE NIGHTS | 35 |
| VISITATIONS | 36 |
| BUILDINGS | 37 |
| SHOPPING | 38 |
| MADNESS | 39 |
| PRESSURE | 40 |
| SANTA CLAUS | 41 |
| LAUNCHING AND DONATIONS | 42 |
| NEW FRIENDS | 43 |
| FOOD AND DRINKS | 44 |
| RENEWAL OF LOVE | 45 |
| HARVESTS | 46 |
| HOUSEWARMING | 47 |
| THANKSGIVINGS | 48 |
| FIGHTS AND TROUBLES | 49 |
| CASES AND JUDGEMENTS | 50 |
| POISONING | 51 |
| PROGRAMS | 52 |
| DANCE BY CHILDREN | 53 |
| MASQUERADES | 54 |
| AGE GRADE INDUCTIONS | 55 |
| PROPOSALS | 56 |
| FAITH | 57 |
| GOD'S PROTECTION | 58 |
| SOME LEARN GAY AND SMOKING | 59 |
| OVERCROWDING LEADING TO RAPE AND INCEST | 60 |
| BORROW POSE | 61 |
| PARTY MOVEMENTS | 62 |

| | |
|---|---|
| CONSTITUTION AMENDMENT | 63 |
| MOONLIGHT TALES | 64 |
| PREGNANCY AND ABORTION | 65 |
| DEATH | 66 |
| ACCIDENTS | 67 |
| EXPENSES | 68 |
| UNNECESSARY WASTE | 69 |
| WAYWARDNESS | 70 |
| NEW YEAR EVE | 71 |
| NEW YEAR | 72 |
| CHRISTMAS | 73 |
| BOXING DAY | 74 |
| THE SEASON | 75 |
| THE REASON | 76 |
| CHRISTIANITY | 77 |
| RELIGION | 78 |
| COOKING | 79 |
| MAIDS | 80 |
| GUARDS | 81 |
| SECURITY MEN | 82 |
| DRINKS | 83 |
| FAMILIES | 84 |
| RENEWAL OF ALTARS | 85 |
| SHIPPING | 86 |
| IMPORTATION | 87 |
| ORDERS | 88 |
| NEW INVENTIONS | 89 |
| SYPHONING PEOPLE | 90 |
| LOSS | 91 |
| ABDUCTION OF BABIES | 92 |
| MOCKERY | 93 |

| | |
|---|---|
| GOSSIP | 94 |
| RUMOURS | 95 |
| SPONSORS | 96 |
| NEW STYLES AND FASHIONS | 97 |
| UPGRADES IN DECORATION | 98 |
| COLOURS EVERYWHERE | 99 |
| BALLOONS | 100 |
| REALITIES | 101 |
| MOMENTS | 102 |
| NEW CULTURES AND TRADITIONS | 103 |
| KNOCKOUTS AND FIREWORKS | 104 |
| JANUARY | 105 |
| EMBRACING THE NEW YEAR | 106 |
| NEW RENT | 107 |
| NEW HOUSE | 108 |
| SEARCHING FOR NEW JOBS | 109 |
| LEAVING OLD BOYFRIENDS FOR NEW ONES | 110 |
| FAKE LIFE | 111 |
| DESPERATION | 112 |
| LOOSENESS | 113 |
| CARELESSNESS | 114 |
| THE AIR | 115 |
| THE RUSH | 116 |
| AS IF IT WILL NEVER COME AGAIN | 117 |
| MISTAKES AND REGRETS | 118 |
| UNNECESSARY DEMANDS | 119 |
| BLACK FRIDAY | 120 |
| CHRIST'S BIRTH | 121 |
| HAPPY CHRISTMAS | 122 |

# Christmas Fever

## JINGLES

Gradually, it comes
The time of the celebrations
Jingles every now and then
Singing of Jesus' birth.

Jingles with lovely tunes
Telling tales of the saviour's birth
Painting stories of good tidings.

Jingles welcoming the saviour
The poor redeemer in manger
With lots of love to shower.

Jingles, beautiful songs and sounds
Powerful tunes and melodies
Excellent messages of Christmas,
Telling tales of Jesus' birth.

Jingles, jingles, Christmas jingles
Stories, tales, songs, movies, dances
Concerts, dramas, plays, compositions
Colours, colourful, wonders, wonderful
Beauty, beautiful, mercy, merciful
Tidings of our saviour's birth
Dawn of mankind's hope and salvation.

## WEATHER AND ATMOSPHERE

The weather changes
The atmosphere radiates,
Glowing in newness and change.

Winter, harmattan, coldness
Dryness and dustiness
Snow, snowing, mist, dews
Showers of fog, thick clouds,
Announcing Christmas.

Cool breeze, sweet sleep
Coiling, rolling on bed
Warm and warm house
Gadgets and heaters
Sweaters and warmers
Telling tales of new season.
Dusty wind, dry weather
Strange atmosphere, yet known
Hopes and wishes for Christmas
Eagerness, curiosity, anxiety
Dreams and desires rising
Christmas fever heating up.

## SEASONS' GREETINGS

Yes, it is time again
Time for seasons' greetings
The seasons are here again.

Greetings from far and wide
From families and friends,
From foes and enemies.

Colleagues throw it around
Lovers fly it in the air
Acquaintances spread it
Rivals blow it
The seasons are here.

Time to celebrate
Time to merry
Colours and jingles
Merriments, everywhere.

Seasons' greetings
Cards, streets, clothing
Messages, actions, celebrations
Seasons' greetings, loud and clear.

## NEW PRODUCTS

Time for new products
Products from nooks and crannies
Serving different purposes.

New products, flooding markets
Cheap, expensive, average
Inferior, superior, fake, original
New products, in and out.

Old ones rebranded
New ones, unbranded
Imitations, look-alikes, same purposes
All for Christmas fever.

High, very high, the fever
Hot, very hot, the temperature
Everyone engrossed
North, south, east, west
Helter-skelter, they run
Celebrating, merrying
In cheers, in pains, in joy, in pretense
Christmas fever in the air.

## RITUALS

Christmas fever on the rise
Catching up with almost everyone
Forcing people to go crazy
Crazy beyond boundaries.

Rituals on the rise
Religious, occultic and others
Sacrifices of different types
Blood, flesh, human, idols.

Killings, missing, kidnappings
Societies and fraternities
Reaching out in diverse forms
Atoning for many things
Refreshing, rekindling, igniting
Dwindling, demoralizing, putting off
Countless activities to be long.

Ritualistic rites by ritualists
Unthinkable acts and stories
Recklessness, wickedness, heartlessness
Ritualization to gain many things
Fever due to Christmas.

## PROSTITUTION

The Christmas fever is high
On and advancing rapidly
Causing lots of things to happen.

The wind of Christmas is here
Blowing up hearts and heads
Swelling and filling them up,
Forcing them to think longer.

Prostitution on the rise
More prospects and customers
Competitions and tactics
Techniques, methods and styles
Prostitutes, not sparing chances.

Urge to get more looks
Hairdos, weavens, attachments
Watches, bracelets, bangles, anklets
Clothing, underwear, vacations
Desperate moves to get perishable things
Diseases notwithstanding
Risks, deaths, tortures, not minding
Prostitution, on the rise
From Christmas fever.

## STEALING

Thieves moving up and down
Pick pockets re-strategizing
Stealing even needlessly.

Stealing on the rise
As Christmas wind blows
Fevers go up and down.

Stealing of all kinds
In many places and times
Ungodly, odd and even.

Even stealing that kills
Dangers and people involved
Places and persons around
They steal, they harden
Not minding whatever.

Christmas fever in the air
Charging, recharging and changing things
Compelling numerous acts
Invoking actions and activities
Fever, hot, running down the spine.

## LIES

Lies, of diverse magnitudes
Both unnecessary and weighty ones
In a bid to manoeuvre.

Manipulators and scavengers
Users and abusers, combining
Tearing up to dupe and betray.

Lies, from the pit of hell
Gearing towards destruction
Only for selfish interests
Bent on deceit and dismay.

Lies, from men and women
Young, and old, children too
In desperation for something
In anticipation for profit,
No matter how lustful.

Husbands lying to wives
Wives lying to husbands
Children lying to parents
Parents lying to children,
Friends and families lying.

Shameful, shameless, shamefully, shamelessly
Liars, lying unnecessarily
Bunch of dead conscience
With nothing to regret of it.

## BUSINESS

The Christmas fever is great
It is always running high
Unveiling new things.

Businesses loom and boom
Swinging and tearing apart
Swelling and swallowing.

Businesses of all kinds
Good, bad, ugly, beautiful
Small and big risks
Large profits, thin losses
Large losses, thin profits
And whatever doable.

Businesses, legal and illegal
Local, national, international
Domestic and foreign
New and old ones
Original and imitations.

Men and women, in and out
Just rushing, eager and ready
The fever of Christmas
Everybody wants to partake.

## PRICES OF GOODS

As rush increases
The prices skyrocket
Demand and supply.

Less supply, high price
High demand, high price
Scarcity, hoarding, high price.

Everyone needs it, yes
Everyone wants it
Even when everyone loves it not.

Prices of goods double
Services drop, yet prices increase
Helter-skelter, they run
Desperation, urgency, passion
Now or never, the fever is on.

Goods, common and ordinary
Goods, uncommon and extraordinary
Goods, normal and reachable
Yet, prices triple,
Sometimes and some areas.

## TRAVEL ARRANGEMENTS

And they begin to prepare
So many things to be arranged
As the fever rages.

Within States, countries
Within borders, along
From country to country,
Preparations and arrangements.

People begin travel documentation
They update and renew, or get
They upgrade their papers
Buy tickets and book airlines
They take dates that suit them
According to their holidays, leaves and pleasures.

They link up with fellow travelers
Relatives, friends, colleagues
They harmonize their movements
And pick times depending on locations.

Christmas fever can be fun
The fever is normal as the year ends,
Yet, abnormal and incredible.

## PREPARATIONS

People at home expect visitors
Be they related or not,
They include miscellaneous.

Preparations from top to down
Renovations and cleanings
New furniture, new utensils
Changes in places necessary.

Washings, beddings, paintings
Arrangements, refurbishments
Sunning, fumigation, weeding
Putting everything in place
As the seasons arrive gradually.

Preparations, especially for occasions too
Numerous outings, sightseeing
Meetings, marriages, burials
Memorials, dances, celebrations
For many buying, expenses
Long list of expenditures
Even when the resources are limited.

## PRAYERS AND CRUSADES

As time advances and draws near
The fever increases
Calling forth so many things
Physically, spiritually and otherwise.

Forces grow, and combat
Alignments and collisions
Disagreements and repulsions
Fights, wars and competitions.

Fortifications and imitations
Sanctifications and consecrations
Desecration and alterations
Prayers, crusades, evangelism.

Secretly, openly, invisible, visible
Known, unknown, real and fake
Businesses and luring
Duping and abracadabra
Enchantments and divinations
Projections and postulations
Prayers upon prayers
As the fever grows.

## DUPING

People device strategies
Means and ungodly ways
Tactics and horrible methods
Just to dupe others.

They dupe whoever
Within and without,
They dupe as many as possible
Not minding the consequences.

High rate of duping
Just to form rich or wealthy
To deceive friends and colleagues,
To feel a sense of belonging
At the detriment of others.

They dupe of monies and properties
They dupe of gold and silver
They set up and entice
They seduce, and rape people,
And do away with their possessions
Because of the season around
To show off and display.

## KIDNAPPING

Kidnappers on rampage
Taking advantage of every chance
Cashing in and out of opportunities
Spoils on the rise.

Men, women, and children
Rich and poor, victims, anyone
Demanding ransoms from and for old and young
Killing unfortunate victims even after ransoms.

Kidnapping for the sake of Christmas
Making money out of evil
Setting traps here and there
Giving people ill luck and fever.

They make huge monies
Suffering people beyond imagination
Traumas, dramas shocks and fevers
Heartlessness at its prime.

They kidnap whoever wherever at any cost
They also have apex victims
Life is nothing to them anymore.

## CRIMES

Crimes, crimes, crimes
They climb outrageously.

Crime, all kinds and manner
New, old, old and new
Evil strategies, ungodly patterns
Real tactics, fake news.

Criminals, new and old
Hardened and mean
Wicked, fearless, godless
They go all out to devour.

Stealing, killing, duping, robbing
Pickpocketing, kidnapping, prostitution
Lying, partners in crime, they are much.

Crimes, from least to most
One by one, bit by bit
Group by group, day by day
The fever harms, the fever hurts
Criminals and their gangs
Criminality, corking and cracking everywhere
Inflicting pain, unleashing mayhem, wrecking havoc.

## MOVEMENTS

Movements increase, humans, vehicular, livestock
The roads get busier
Traffics get thicker
And longer, the journeys.

Costs of transportation
Expenses and expenditures.

Movements in different forms
North, south, east and west
Diverse reasons, times and modes
By land, sea and air.

Cargoes, in and out
Humans, up and down.

They move, they move
They go, they return, more frequently
Busy roads, busy routes
Busy life, busy humans
Greater risks, greater gains
Bountiful doubts and fears
Time and chance happen to them all.

## CONGESTIONS

Yes, congestions and crowds
In markets, and roads
Airports, railways, stations
Arrivals and departures.

Rowdiness and overcrowded-ness
Noises, nuisances, busyness
Carelessness, pressure and heat.

Congestions in religious places
Parks, fields, amenities
Stress, strain, push
Wears and tears, fears.

More demands, more supply
Less supply, maybe more demand
More demands, maybe less supply
Stretches and overstretches.

Congestions and contradictions
Constipation and conscription
Construction and compression
Excess and excessive use
The Christmas fever
Red, hot, harsh and hovering.

## LAND SPECULATIONS

They put up many things
Because of home-comers
The ones that are visiting
To have a cruise and fly.

They speculate lands
They dupe some
They hike some
They hike prices
They sell same to many
They cause troubles many a time.

The Christmas fever
So hot, very hot
Heating up the land
Harming some, hurting some
Healing some, helming some.

They sell at give away too
Sometimes they are real
Because of urgency and emergency.

Land speculators, and speculations
They have done more harm than good.

## SUITORS AND ARRANGEMENTS

Christmas fever, real and fake
Suitors pouring in and out,
Some serious, some unserious.

Arrangements going on
Men and women arranging
Ladies and gentlemen, preparing
Preparing to meet suitors.

Mothers and fathers, parents
Picking, selecting, fixing
Matchmaking, looking out for the best
Getting their children hooked.

Suitors in their numbers
Brides numerous,
Yet, confusion and doubts.

Reasons and reasons
Criteria, time and background
Cultures and religions
Behaviours, beliefs and dreams
Suitors, brides to be, around
The Christmas fever, really hot.

## MARRIAGES

Many marriages go on
Cultural, traditional, foreign
In different areas and locations.

Some emergency, some planned
Old and young, rich and poor
Clans, families, villages
Communities, lands and climes.

Marriages, colourful and beautiful
Dry and wet, few and many
Plenty and scanty, everywhere.

People marry, they merry
They celebrate and party
Prayers, wishes and wills
Marriages of many types.

The Christmas fever
Coming with challenges
Challenges of all kinds
Finance, time, strength, power
Will, choice, zeal, resources
Means, abilities, capabilities, capacities.

## MEETINGS

Lots and lots of meetings
Males, females, both
Unions, families and towns
Youths, children and general.

Separate, collective
Cultural and religious
Arms, units and divisions
Meetings in hierarchies.

Organizations, societies
Social institutions
Departments, branches
Home and abroad.

Meetings on so many topics
X-raying problems and solutions
Looking for better chances
Mapping out lasting solutions and strategies.

Making new rules and regulations
Suggestions and objections
Objectives and activities
Events and occasions,
The Christmas fire burning.

## ABROAD GUYS

They come in their numbers
From abroad they fly in
They look flashy and crazy
They display big abroad-ness.

Gold, silver, diamond
Earrings, chains, necklaces
Anklets, wrist watches
Designer wears and shoes
Cars and accessories
They look good and wealthy
Even on borrowed riches.

They toast girls and ladies
They flirt around
They promise heaven
But sometimes, they give hell.

Careless, wayward, casual, reckless
Mean, ruthless, promiscuous
They play around and go
Some disappear forever.

They deceive a lot of girls
They frustrate in-laws to be
They push aside serious suitors,
Christmas fevers, hot and hotter.

## VILLAGE PEOPLE

Village people, yes, everyone
We all come from there
No matter how polished we become.

Village people, crude and raw
Also waiting for abroad-ians
Prepared, ready and set
Hoping, longing, expecting, praying.

The Christmas fever, hot and hotter
Village people getting hotter along
Never ready to be intimidated.

Preparations, readiness, prayers
Excitements, enthusiasm
Happiness and cautiousness
The village people advance.

Forces of different types
Striking for and against
Together and or in disarray
Pressures and collisions
Commotions, commitments and exploitations
The Christmas fever touches all.

## PRIDE SHOWS

Pride and display of shows
Pomposity and arrogance
 Complex, inferiority and superiority
All in full battle for self.

Pride from the pit of hell
Pride above skyscrapers
Cranes and pinnacles, high
Shows meet them up there.

Poor and haggard fellows
Timid and rural souls
Archaic and backward heads
In competition with all.

Rich people climbing up
Stepping on toes, fingers
Scraping feelings and thoughts
Only for self to be elevated.

The Christmas fever towering
Collecting beacons of humility
Shattering walls of lowliness
In a world of shameful shame.

## BURIALS

Burials also take place
Whether they died then or now
No matter their age.

Burials of some elders
Or even the young
Intentionally fixed them
Or unavoidably fixed now.

Burials, expensive or cheap
Aged or tender, man or woman
Competitions of madness
Madness of no rivalry,
Yet madness of rivalries.

Burials are for mourning
Death is no fun
Loss is loss, no matter what
Yet, monies are wasted.

As the living mourn in hunger
Monies for better things go into it
Christmas fever, fever indeed
A time of unexplainable craziness.

## FOOTBALL COMPETITIONS

Matches and marches
Football tournaments
Stadia, stadium, fields, open spaces,
Parks, pitches, camps and arenas.

Individual sponsorship
Communal sponsorship
General entertainment
Talent hunts and scouting
Championships in grades.

Football competitions
Home and abroad players
Gathering at Christmas season
To play, merry, cheer, fan
They have fun under one umbrella.

Tournaments of several prizes
Challenges and winners
Warmness of home, unity of base.

Troubles arise sometimes
Fights, disputes, disagreements
Partiality, bribery, corruption, match fixing
Football competitions, wonders, wondrous involvement.

## CEREMONIES

Ceremonies abound
Burials, weddings, dedications
Child naming, housewarming
Thanksgivings, foundation laying.

Invited and uninvited guests
Friends and well-wishers
Rivals, colleagues, visitors
Strangers, enemies, relatives.

Crusades, dances, festivals
Age grades and age groups
All kinds of ceremonies
Fuming, foaming, framing in the hotness
The hotness of Christmas fever.

Parades, maidens, and warriors
Virgins, aged, young and mid age
Godly and ungodly ceremonies
Carnivals, troupes, artists
Melody and harmony, many
Colourful and wonderful moments
Fever, heat, the atmosphere is great.

## SIGHTSEEING

Yes, teeming population
As friends and families gather
From all walks of life
Different bases and exposures
They meet at home again.

From time to time, old places
Schools, parks, streams, farms
Churches, markets, town squares
Maternal and paternal homes
They move around histories.

Sightseeing with relatives
With children, families
Telling stories, refreshing memories
Creating history, making friends
The Christmas season is great
The lessons and tidings amaze.

## REUNIONS

Great opportunity to meet again
Reunions of great and small
Old relatives and old friends
People long forgotten and seen
A time to reunite in love.

Peace, bonding harder
Love, growing stronger
Unity, towering higher
Tides, spreading faster
Time, holding them dear.

Reunions, students and teachers
Unions of green lands
Friendship of souls and minds
Relationship of soundness
Seasons of beautiful reasons
The Christmas fever is not in vain.

Reunions of luxurious abode
Circles and cycles of bonds
Speaking greater things than of old.

## MEMORIALS

A lot of memorials
Great, grand and great grand parents
Brothers and sisters
Aunts and uncles
Relatives, friends and well wishers.

Monuments in their honour
Donations on their behalves
Pledges and promises
Foundations and grand breaking events.

Memorials, high and low
General, individual, family
Collective, communal and state
Memorials, honourable.

Gatherings and prayers
Memorials, stories, lectures, events
Speeches, highlights and awards
Memories, memorials, great and great.

A time for tributes and celebrations
In honour of the dead or the living,
The Christmas fever, all around.

## GIFTS

Gifts, in and out
Up and down, around
In different forms and sizes
Colours, shapes and shades.

Materials, monies, promises
Foodstuffs, perfumes, clothing
Toiletries, shoes, necklaces, rings, beads
Gold, silver, diamond, bronze
In whatever form and face.

Gifts in diverse forms
From different people
To different people.

The rich, the poor, the average
The orphan, orphanages, the less privileged
Organizations and groups
Individuals, friends, colleagues, colleges
Associates, partners, cliques and others.

Gifts in their numbers
Even foods and drinks
The Christmas season is amazing.

## LATE NIGHTS

Late nights, yes, in and out
Movements, to and fro
Chats, discussions, meetings
Leisure, plays, long memories.

Traffic, crowds, congestions
Storytelling and merrymaking
Friends and families in jolly-ment
Partying in love and happiness.

Late nights, staying awake for long
Watching television, listening to news
Seeing movies, cinemas
A natural delaying of sleep.

Warmness and warm-heartedness
Excitements and comeliness
Remembrances and jokes
Laughs, Laughter, and smile.

Near or far, around or not
The heat of togetherness
The freedom of movement
And the reality of such gatherings
Christmas is a time of times.

## VISITATIONS

Visitations, on and off
Strangers and visitors
Relatives, friends and friends of friends
Gifts, cash and kind
From visitors to visitors
From the visited to visitors
From strangers , all and sundry.

Planned visitations
Unplanned visitations
Meetings and Telepathies
Coincidences, chances and luck
Programmed and coordinated
Unprogrammed and uncoordinated.

Homes, houses, parks, fields
Tours, sightseeing, mountain climbing
Alma maters, camps and other places
The Christmas fever burns red.

Prayers, solemn assemblies
Dances, events, occasions,
Visits, visitors, visitations, visiting
The season is one so unique.

## BUILDINGS

Buildings, type by type
Houses, here and there
Erections, one by one
Many, numerous, like that.

Buying lands and properties
Kicking them off, at once
Foundation laying, ceremonies
Primary, secondary or others.

Foundations, halfway
Midway, finishing touches
Packing in, housewarming
In a twinkle, all is done.

Building, towers, miracles
Gigantic and wonderful
Only determination does it.

Time for reflection, decision
Searches, searching
Thorough observation in short time
Great conclusion and results,
The fever is very hot.

## SHOPPING

Time to shop, shopping and shipping
Shipping and shipping too
In many lands and climes
For various reasons and gains.

High demand, high cost
More production, imitations
Quest for satisfaction
Shopping abounding.

Bonus and bonanza
Discounts and promotions
Deceits and subterfuge
Camouflage and sabotage,
Rigmaroles, the fever rises.

Shopping, men and women
Buying, old and young
Rush, seed, urge, eagerness
Competitions and struggles
Everyone to their fate
Advancing to take advantage
Adventures, so complicated
Discoveries, so complex.

## MADNESS

Madness in the air
Insanity flying around.

Unnecessary pressure around
Extraordinary forces zooming
Enlarging coasts of trouble
And squeezing tents of peace.

Madness, type by type
Real and fake, strong
Manmade and artificial
Preventable and avoidable
Lust, quest, greed, selfishness.

Full moon, monthly, seasonal
Ritualistic madness and kinds
Envious, jealous, dubious breed
The ones taken advantage of.

People routed and caged
Bottled and terminated
Those useless-ed, abused, dumped
Because of the fever,
Or whatever known or unknown.

## PRESSURE

Pressure from everywhere
Within and without
Peer pressure, societal, cultural
Martial, religious, general
Pressures that should not be.

Pressure from around
Work, family, past and present
Pressure, for and or against future
Torments, seen and unseen
Intimidation, lurking around.

Scarcity, lack, want, need
Poverty, hate, anger, wretchedness
Pressure, dismantling peace.

Personal and public pressure
Depression, disappointments and loss
Forces of unbargained outcomes
Fears of bargained results
Taunting hands of times
Daunting the good, the bad, the ugly.

The fever is high, higher than normal
Taking long to cool,
If it ever does.

## SANTA CLAUS

Santa Claus in town
Near, seen, perceived
Yet far, unseen, unknown.

The favourite saint of children
With gifts to please them
Yet, they pay for it.

In red and white
Looking big and scary
Yet, beautiful and handsome
Santa, fantasizes the children.

But then, there is a reality
The reality of lies
Lies, the only truth.

Let it be told, yes tell it
Tell it that Santa is a fraud
A fraud from authorities
Authorities that shrink the people.

The Christmas fever is real
But then, Santa Claus is here,
Here to gift everyone.

## LAUNCHING AND DONATIONS

Launchings, up and down
In nooks and crannies
Donations, loud and clear
In groups and organizations.

Duping, more and more
Launching, fake and real
Some launch in millions
Some as millionaires
Taking name and fame
Showing glory and honour
Yet, never fulfilling any.

Forced, compelled launchers
Coerced donors and givers
Murmurs and murmurings
Pain and display of wealth,
Show, nonsense and mannerless.

Launchings to steal
Launchings to kill
Money, love of money
The root of all evil.

## NEW FRIENDS

As people travel up and down
They meet new people
Strangers far and near
And some turn friends.

Some meet in airports, airlines
Some meet at parks, terminals
Some in rail stations, heliports
Some meet at wharfs
Some inside cabs, taxis, buses
Some in planes, roads, routes
In traffic, stoppages, branches
Locals, nationals , foreigners.

New friends, we meet
As the fever boils hot
Or even cools off.

Strangers save, help, marry
They become closer like families
They change so many things
Some however, can turn cruel.

## FOOD AND DRINKS

So many merriment
Enjoyment galore, fun
Foods and drinks, partying.

Their prices top up, their demand increases
More flood the market
Competitions and rivalries
Choices and confusions
We log in to the fever and time.

Foods and drinks, chilled
Hot, warm, wherever, however
Served, services, satisfactions
People wander and dabble.

Assorted foods and drinks
In homes, homes of the rich
All kinds according to taste and test
People controlling stores and parks.

However, some thirst and hunger
Wishing, wanting, needing, lacking
Longing, praying, hoping, dying
The fever burns them down.

## RENEWAL OF LOVE

Yes, some renew their love
As they meet after a long time
They rededicate themselves
Renew their vows and covenants.

Love glows anew
Shinning and dazzling
As if it only just began.

Out of sight, out of mind
Out of memory and flesh
Bone to bone, flesh to flesh
Ordinances revive naturally.

No matter the time and chance
The change and faults
The pain and agony
Love finds its way
Piercing the heart
And penetrating through
Because the fever is Christmas.

## HARVESTS

And churches fix harvest
Family, village, individual
Communal, general harvests
They come with cash and kind.

Harvest in all shades
Forms of appreciation
In your fields of life
People from all walks of life.

Harvests and harvesters
Dancing in to the throne of God
With thanksgiving and rejoicing.

Fruits from our farm
Seeds from our barn
Plenty and bounty
In pureness of heart
And newness of life.

Numerous gifts and praises
Showing oneself unto God
In the presence of their maker.

## HOUSEWARMING

Many new houses built
Ready for dedication,
Housewarming and openings
Guests, writers and visitors
Friends, relatives, families
All joining in the ceremony.

Big ceremony, all day long
Happiness and merriment
Jubilations and testimonies
Incredible stories and talks
Wining and dining, jolly-ing.

People travel far and wide
In honour of friends,
To partake in good things
To support, cheer, respect.

Housewarming, in many places
Too many occasions
Noises, sounds, music
Rhythm and soul, sanity
Movements of glow and show.

## THANKSGIVINGS

A lot of thanksgiving
From all and sundry
Men and women
Youths and children,
Different arms, groups and organizations.

Dedication and rededication
Thanksgivings, presentations
Villages, towns
Turn by turn, collectively.

Thanksgivings, for survivals
End of year parties,
Symposiums, get together
Sendoffs and sendforths
Welcome parties, goodbyes.

Thanksgiving unto God
For His mercies, care, protections
Safeguards, guidance, blessing
Forgiveness, cleansing and sanctification,
Thanksgiving for promotion
For healing, childbirth, and marriages.

So many things to be thankful for
Too many reasons to praise God,
The Christmas fever, adoration unto God too.

## FIGHTS AND TROUBLES

As people move around
Chances of everything increase,
Fights and troubles
Disagreement, exchange of words
Abuses, verbal and physical too.

Crowd, congestion, competition
Intimidation, rivalry, belittlement
Personal, general, communal
Clashes, conflicts, differences
Confusions, commotions, contemplation.

Slight irritations, deep brushing
Physical contacts, bruises
Combats, quarrels, jealousy
Families, kindred, clans,
Fights and troubles, on the rise.

They can be curtailed too
Yes, they can be averted
Different folks, different strokes
The Christmas fever boils.

## CASES AND JUDGEMENTS

The ruins heaped
Fixed dates for judgement
Old cases already picked.

Cases from old and new
Judgements to be rendered
For, against, neutral.

Lobbies, lobbying, lobbyist
Bribery, influences, alterations
Parties, classes and groups
Oppositions, affiliates, support.

Painted lies, coated words
Sugary tales, sweet stories
Guilty, guiltless, innocent, in wave
The waves blow, the storms rage.

Cold wars, hot arguments
Blind reality, raw manipulations
Crude tactics, advanced tricks
The Christmas fever boils
Boiling in diverse ways for different purposes.

## POISONING

Evil people on rampage
Like lions and wildlife,
Seeking for whom to devour
Going about doing harm
Inflicting pain and curse
Tearing people down
Pulling down pillars
Crushing stars and destinies,
Twisting fates and dimming lights.

Evil hearts, bitter souls, angry folks
Even unoffended ones
Some friends, some enemies
Some rivals, some partners.

They pretend sometimes
They come close sometimes
They play hide and seek,
They appear friendly
They flow with the go
And go with the flow,
Only to lay in wait
Like adders and scorpions
To kill, to harm, to crush, to sting
The Christmas fever blows
Hot, cold, up, down
Blowing east, west, north, south
Careless, irrespective of who is involved.

## PROGRAMS

Programs, all types and shades
Religious, cultural, political
Social, educational, traditional
In and out, home and abroad
Far and near, wide and reach.

Programs, good and entertaining
Mourning, mournful, meaningful, meaningless
Old and new ones
Useful and useless ones.

Youths, children, men and women
Humans, intra, inter
Lone, ultra, extra
Crude and digital.

Programs, supported, supportive
Opposed, purposed, proposed, purposeful
Individual, collective
Expensive and cheap types
Moral, spiritual, intellectual
All nooks and crannies,
Different intents and motives
Ulterior, utmost, upper, power, lower.

The Christmas fever is a furnace
Burning with flames,
Flames of wonders.

## DANCE BY CHILDREN

Children dance around
They make traditional uniforms
And move from place to place
Dancing for people,
To entertain and gain
They earn gifts and money.

People even strangers love them
They dash them money
In the end of some weeks
They share their income
And each use theirs as wish.

They start this, some days to Christmas
And stop before or after the new year
This particular dance is occasional
Because of the Christmas fever.

Children of different ages, sizes and shapes
They have dressers and patrons
Their parents support them, too
And they are mostly girls.

## MASQUERADES

Masquerades, many types
This is especially for boys
They mask themselves too,
Going around dancing, entertaining
And also getting some cash.

Little boys from different homes
Their team has a name
They have uniforms sometimes
They go about during Christmas
They dance and entertain
And make some money too.

They are like troupes
They can be hired too
They go in and out of town
Their sight alone is funny
And their dance lovely.

Masquerades and masquerade boys
They are equivalent to the girls' group,
Except the girls are not masquerades
Christmas fever, high and low.

## AGE GRADE INDUCTIONS

Age grade groups too
They hold meetings and ceremonies
Get together, end of year party
Condolences, chieftainship
And inductions into the group.

Age by age, grade by grade
Time by time, group by group
Mate by mate, batch by batch
Name by name, mission by mission
Big ceremonies and celebrations.

Rules, laws, regulations, stipulations
Order, respect, discipline
Boundaries, constitutions
Members must be loyal to
And abide by them all.

Age grade inductions
Family and friends, villages
Communities and neighbours
So many people partake in the ceremony
Whether during Christmas or not
But the fever is on.

## PROPOSALS

A lot of proposals
Job, contract, marriage
Promises, pledges, commitments
Covenants, introductions, meetings
Chances, opportunities, dates
Proposals upon proposals
Real ones fake ones, deceits
Trial and error, hit and run
Different opportunities calling.

Proposals in line, online, offline
Suggestions, possible and impossible
Opinions, great and small
Plans, soft and hard
Plots, good and bad
Chances, slim and thick
Agreements, loose and tight
Outcomes, disastrous and encouraging.

Proposals, first party, second party, third party
Everyone with their personal interest.

## FAITH

Some people do not celebrate Christmas
They say their faith forbids it
So they stay away from the razzmatazz
Yet they travel around Christmas.

They fix occasions and programs
They meet and greet people
They join in sightseeing
Yet, their faith forbids it.

They marry, they wed, they bury
They merry, they mourn, they gather
They do all things during this time
They partake in some occasions
Because during this period, people return
Home and abroad, far and near.

They make new clothes, dresses
They make new hair, hair styles
They build new houses and park into them
They celebrate like others and with them
Yet, their faith forbids it
The Christmas fever is hot.

## GOD'S PROTECTION

People seeking protection
Left, right, front, back, center
Seeking power here and there
Taking cover openly and secretly
Hiding laughably like the ostrich.

Protection from spirits against spirits
Protection from men against men
Protection from women against women,
Protection from funny places against funny reasons.

Some being deceived by prophets
Some false prophets and bad seers
Visioners of ungodly eyes
Duping and defrauding desperate people,
And even the innocent, ignorant people.

In the end, if God is not involved
All is vain, vanity upon vanity.

God's protection is sure
Nothing tears it down
It expires only when God withdraws
Stay glued, stay tuned to Him
Before, after, during Christmas fever.

## SOME LEARN GAY AND SMOKING

Peer pressure rises then
As characters travel around and mix
The good, the bad, the ugly
With more freedom due to activities.

Some learn homosexuality
Some turn lesbians
Some start smoking
Some embrace alcoholism
Some begin womanizing
All sorts of vices, topple.

Innocent looking, pure and poor
Humble, young and green
Ignorant and inarticulate
Only for a careless hour to slip off.

Criminality moving and lurking around
Capturing tender minds and hearts
Destroying people, souls and heads
Because the Christmas fever is burying.

Poor ones trying to fit in
Feeble knees breaking in pieces
Because of Christmas pressure.

## OVERCROWDING LEADING TO RAPE AND INCEST

As people move from place to place
We meet characters
And forces pull us apart or together.

Overcrowding in parks, fields
Houses, homes, religious places
Streams, farms, and everywhere
Sometimes, left alone
And chances of ill rise.

Even relatives can harm
Friends too, can
Strangers do of course,
Though, they can be angels.

Rape and lust lure youths
Although not only youths,
When many people sleep together
Or stay so close in a strange place,
Without checks and balances,
Things may go out of hand
Due to overcrowding.

Even incest, happen
Urges rise and stain,
After awhile it clears
And then, the deed is done.

The Christmas fever is real
It catches across borders
If not properly checked.

## BORROW POSE

Because Christmas is near
People feel intimidated
They do ungodly things
Just to feel a sense of belonging.

They borrow so many things
Either to return later intact,
Or pay back with interest
They pledge and promise weird things
Things, they may have trouble meeting up.

Some borrow clothes and shoes
Some borrow money and jewels
Some borrow cars and bikes
Just to entice girls and friends
To prove to people how rich they are
To pass the wrong message
To portray a false image,
Unfortunately deceiving themselves;
Self deceit, the worst.

The fever of Christmas is harsh
It can get the innocent trapped,
And the poor, fooled.

## PARTY MOVEMENTS

Party movements up and down
Dress codes, weird and crazy
People, restless and excited
Waiting to kill and be killed.

Party movements in all areas
Politics, social, finance, education
Culture, tradition, and all
They gather, they compete
They collide and clash,
Conflict of interests
Similarities and differences.

Party, party, partners
Personal, parties and public
Movements and struggles
Struggles and movements,
Noise, shows and empty displays.

Secret and open movements
Tactical, public, private, cabals
Crews, executives and general
The fever rages on and on.

## CONSTITUTION AMENDMENT

When people come home
They make new rules
And face new dawn,
As new beginnings
Hoping for a good future.

They make new laws and rules
They set new committees
And reshuffle or change their leaders
They move with trends,
As times and trials advance.

They embrace change
Positive change for the society
The change for the futures.

Amended laws and rites
New methods and patterns
Lasting solutions, sustainable goals
Hopes and ways forward.

Revisitations of old laws and cultures
Renewal and removal of some customs,
Institution of newness.

# MOONLIGHT TALES

Yes, the moonlight tale
Fairy tales and life experiences
Gathering at catchment areas
Village squares, family squares
Under the trees and shades
Wherever lovely and natural
Under the moonlight.

Tales and togetherness
Having loved ones warmed up,
Keeping families awake
Into the wee hours of the day
As they laugh and play
Whiling away time and pain.

Tales by moonlight
Tales of life and death
Mysteries, jokes, stories
Past, present and future
Teaching, learning, leisure
Hopes, dreams, aspirations
Cautions, prayers, laughter
Regrets, and a whole lot
Tales under moonlight are special.

## PREGNANCY AND ABORTION

As numbers troop in and out
People catch their fancy
Lust and love grow.

Youths explore their might
Adolescents get excited
Teenagers flare up emotions
Adults team up too
All ignorantly, carelessly
Freely, relaxed, confused
And with little or no care.

Things happen, victims go in
Heads roll, unlucky lads
Everyone in the web
Pregnancies come up
Abortion rises, chances grow.

Even relatives fall victims
When lust and ungodliness stir
Aged ones even ride the young
The rich cruise the poor
The great ruin the small
Pregnancies roll up and roll in,
Which may lead to abortion
And unhygienic ones may take lives
Or cause diseases severely.

## DEATH

Yes, even death occurs
In double or triple folds
Avoidable deaths at that.

Food poisoning, fights, crashes
Clashes, conflicts, carelessly
Rivalry, and anything that may come up.

Death, in any field
At anywhere
Careless and wayward play
In the streams, parks
Sightseeing, from arguments
And minor or major disagreements,
From football tournaments
From commonest provocation.

Career death, dream death
Physical, spiritual, political
Cultural and any manner of death
People die, lives get lost
During Christmas, because of its fever
Unfortunately, many are preventable
But the fever burns up remedies.

## ACCIDENTS

As movements double
Loads and humans triple
Roads get busier and smaller
Leading to any harm.

Deaths occur untimely
Along deadly roads and routes
Bad roads, decayed, dilapidated
Horrible and horrifying links
Terrible scenes and spots
Ungodly tracks and lanes
Demonic means and methods
Barbaric accidents, horrors.

Crashes and crushes of lives
Humans in bloody pieces
Ignorance, impatience, insecurity
Inexperience, inefficiencies, inhumanity
Accidents, wasting lives, old and young.

Families in pain
Relatives in tears
Friends in dilemma,
Wishes, thoughts, prayers, regrets
Bad government, terrible governance.

Christmas fever, high and up
Raining, reigning, ruining, running,
Torturing, tormenting, tearing
And leaders seated unconcerned.

## EXPENSES

Expenses rise as well
On everything and everywhere
Prices skyrocket even for less goods
Inferior things flood the market
Cheaper ones too, flood.

Expenses gear up more
Glaring so boldly
Staring so proudly
Notwithstanding conditions.

Large families suffer more
Poor homes wail
Average people manage life
Stumbling on stones and potholes.

Less results, less satisfactions
More expectations, more expenditures, more loss
Negative gains, and profits
Recycling wastes and bins
Garnishing troubles and traumas.

Beware of Christmas
And the fever,
For Christmas fever will not just go away.

## UNNECESSARY WASTE

Unnecessary wastes
False living, false hopes
Wasting food and money
Time moving fast
Things getting stuck.

Little and huge wastes
From adults and children
Thinking life is surplus,
Forgetting time fades away.

Food, money, resources
Materials, efforts, results
Rolling up sleeves to dirts.

Wastes, local and foreign
Within and without, near and far
False impression that kills
Deception of self by self
Destruction of mind by mind,
Fooling others and oneself,
Yet, seeing a greenlight.

The Christmas fever boils
Bewitching and bewildering
Consorting and concocting,
Consulting and consuming
Distorting and disturbing
Disrupting and erupting,
Feverish, fevers that last with aftermath.

## WAYWARDNESS

Waywardness increases
Looseness and silliness
Unrestricted movements and advance,
Careless talks and aims
Lustful aids and help
Boundless dates and nights,
Dark adventures and discoveries.

Waywardness, corrupting values
Stinking pigs defecating tracks
Dirty linens covering holes
Holes and holes of crookedness.

Parades and charades of vain
Vanity, trials and errors
Hide and seek, trial by error
Landscapes of death
Dungeons of animalistic journey
Layers of insanity quaking
Waywardness grooming aloud
The Christmas fever, hot and charming.

# NEW YEAR EVE

The new year eve is another
In different places, they bomb
They burn and smoke
Darkness and fire
Fireworks, brightness in the sky.

Tires, plastics, woods
Heavy metals and rags
They gather at junctions
They set them ablaze at roundabouts
A wake, a new dawn
Pollution, nuisance, diseases
Whatever they spread, no one cares.

Noises, jubilations, celebrations
Shouts, vigils, religious rituals
Sacrifices, prayers, incantations
Powers, altars, forces, realms
The new year eve is outrageous.

Still people die, mysteries
In different forms and times
Avoidable and unavoidable deaths
The Christmas fever is really hot.

## NEW YEAR

And the new year arrives
Resolutions flood in and out
Decisions flare up,
Hope rises, dreams build
Aspirations gather together.

The new year looks new
Appearing bright and fresh
Sounding promising and young
Signifying prosperity and happiness,
But then the fear is there.

Wishes, roses, flowers, love
Warm hugs and embraces
Forgone alternatives, opportunity cost
Desires, determinations, strengths
Happiness, joy, newness, faith
The new year proceeds.

But then life goes on
Featuring and fixing us
Serving and saving us
Placing, forcing, blowing
We wonder and wander
As life poses itself on us
And lives in us, as it pleases.

## CHRISTMAS

Christmas comes, awaited
Long, prepared, announced, booked
We merry and play together.

Christmas grows, rolls on
Advancing in redness
Yet green and lively.

Foods, drinks, cakes, gifts
Greetings, gifting, occasions
Children in merriment
Adults in celebrations,
The saviour is born.

Born to rule, to save
A world long gone and destroyed,
A bitter earth, decayed land.

Christmas harnesses joy
The joy of salvation
A poor virgin and manger
A loving redeemer so humble,
Willing and ready to rescue.

## BOXING DAY

The next, the boxing day
A day for gifts
A holiday for gifting and giving.

Some do, some do not
Some remember, some forget
Some appreciate, some never
Some acknowledge, some otherwise.

Some would have given
But have not,
Still nobody gives them.

Some starve, some thirst
Some waste resources
While the poor dwindle.

Boxing day is in the heart
No matter the gifts we give,
For a people, for others
It is done, as a reason,
As the season booms.

## THE SEASON

The season glows
Shining like stars everywhere
Igniting love and wonders
Spreading joy in hearts,
As the happiness is contagious.

But then, some are in pain
They are hungry and angry
They faint and their strength fails
They gasp for air and life
They pray and hope,
They wish and desire
But life seems far.

Answers drive them mad
Reasons get them crazy
Because the season is red.

The Christmas fever, trying
Showing weakness and want
Displaying lack and need
Preaching regrets and bitterness.

## THE REASON

The reason for the season
Our saviour is born
Peace unto the earth
All glory to God on high.

The reason of calmness
The reason to shelter,
The reason to feed and save
The reason to delight
The season of colours
Colours of magical wonder.

Yuletide and Christmas
Seasonal reason, yet global
Global reason, seasonal
Reasonable season
Our saviour is born.

Joy to the world
Let the earth be healed
Let the world be saved
Let the weak be strengthened
And the poor be made rich.

## CHRISTIANITY

Christians and Christianity
As the world celebrates Christmas,
Christianity deepens and brightens
Broadening and widening
Yet suffocating and choking.

Christians, holidaying
But meditations, slipping
True thoughts, sliding.

Christianity in all the lands
Suffering setbacks all round
Physically, spiritually, morally
Mentally, politically, socially
And the gates of hell flooding.

Christians, loose and careless
As forces wrap up the world
Enveloping stars and moons
When they should occupy.

Wars and terrors, terrors and wars
Advancing, tormenting the Christendom,
Hate, racism, greed, selfishness
Lust, pride, ignorance and injustice
All, and many more
Dividing the body of Christ.

## RELIGION

Religion, the birth of rivalry
Rivalries and competitions
Seen and unseen fights
Known and unknown wars
Limits and boundaries,
Borders of hell stones
Worlds of estrangement
Strangling and choking out humanity.

Religion, a piece of pig
Dirtying hearts and souls
Inflicting pain and misery
Confronting peace and harmony
Challenging unity and care
Crushing love and banquets.

Religion, a pin in the throat
A thorn in the heart
A boil on the flesh
Doing more harm than good
Building mansions and paradises
With blood, skulls and lives
Yet appearing holy and peaceful.

Christmas fever along the tides
Times of redness and hotness,
Strands left, unleft
Unmet goals of invisible reasons.,
A raging fever, ravaging.

## COOKING

Cooking changes well
Increment in all branches
Size, quality, time, need
Cooks, chefs, kitchens
Feeders, eaters, groups.

They cook more often
Some intermittently
Quality, service, time
No matter who is involved.

The kitchen gets busier
As visitors and events increase
The quality appreciates
As time and seasons ply
The size enlarges
As people outnumber the old.

Cooking, in and out
Off and on, now and then
Little rest, more work
The Christmas fever is on
Everyone gets involved
It warns the world
Directly or indirectly.

## MAIDS

Maids do more work
They get busier
New roles and new laws
Time gets longer
Because of goods and services.

Some bonus, sometimes
Hard work, hard labour
Joyful though, it may be.

Servants in their numbers
Some also getting holidays
Off and settlements
Compensations and pays
Gifts, in cash and kind
And also for their families sometimes.

Maids, neater, smarter
Faster, lovelier, livelier, stronger, better
Because Christmas is on
As Santa is clean and beautiful
No matter what happens
We all look up to the seasons.

## GUARDS

Guards, male and female
Guards and guards of humans
In uniforms and mufti
Agile, ready, good for work.

They stay, they work
They breeze in and out
If opportunities arise
And visit when duty calls.

They face their work wholly
They man the gates
And their duty posts, stable
They risk it all, all the time.

Their own families look on
Waiting, watching, hoping
Yet, strong for them
Their hearts connect.

All of them hang on
Special people with special strength
One wonders how they cope,
The Christmas fever is hard.

## SECURITY MEN

They are the powerhouse
They guard and guide
Everyone depends on them
Yet, safety is of the Lord.

They fear no death
They must be there
Yet, they die.

They cannot be home
They are at forefront
Steadied at the front lines
They fight insurgencies
They safeguard the land
They protect the borders
They defend and ward off,
They have homes and families.

Security men, high and low
Great and small, no matter how
They risk their life
They live on the line
To shield their own,
Even when it cost their blood.

## DRINKS

Drivers, the road friends
They fly, they sail, they drive
Air, water and land
They are always on route
For a course at a cost.

Despatching information
Delivering goods and services
Dropping men and women
Discharging their duty.

Sometimes, they sleep on roads
With hazards and dangers
They bet life and death
They take whatever comes.

The Christmas fever blows
Blowing like wind and harmattan
So cold, so hot, so warm
Leaving behind doubts and fears
Cropping mixed feelings
Bordering the bothered,
And bothering the bordered too.

## FAMILIES

Families, thousands of them
North, south, east, west
Flying and travelling around,
To celebrate the Christmas.

In happy mood especially
Some in sad, due to loss
Yet, the family-ness is there.

Families, rich and poor
Great and small
Known and unknown
Learned, unlearned, global
They frolic in hardworking
Sharing in joy of the season.

Families praying together
Merrying and partying
Missing loved ones
Crowning relatives, friends
Worshipping their lord high
As the fever entwines,
Season in, season out.

## RENEWAL OF ALTARS

Family altars revive
Altars, long, lonely
Sustaining shrines
Points of meeting
Places of covenants
Cross of oaths and offerings.

Renewal of altars
Family ties get warmed
People and warmness
Voices, gifts and melodies
Songs of exaltation
Sacrifices of Thanksgiving.

In and out, far and wide
People renew altars
They revive forces
For and against,
Proposing, opposing
Altars grow, altars clash
They surmount, and destroy
But the Christmas altar is gold
The one raising the fever.

## SHIPPING

Shipping multiplies
By people, individuals, companies
Nations, organizations, networks
Businesses boom, all kinds.

Cost also rises, profit and loss
Across borders, lands and seas
Offshore, onshore, Mediterranean
Caribbean, Sahara,
Goods and services, move
Men and women, need.

Clothes, shoes, oil, cars, creams
Perfumes, toiletries, building materials
Wrappers, metals, ammunitions
Legal, illegal, smugglers
Pirates, piracy, disturbances
Even human trafficking
Organ harvesting and harvesters
Ritualists, everything on the suspect.

The Christmas fever is real
Hot and high on humans
Injustice and inhumanity growing
Catching up with hate.

## IMPORTATION

Importation climbs mountains
Scaling through walls, pillars and fences
Leaning on columns and beams
Trashing ceilings and roofs
Yet, hindering a lot.

Importation of foods and fruits
Edibles and perishable
Importation of tangible and intangible
Hard, soft, clean and dirty.

Chains and cells
Rings and webs
Networks and links
Importation; contrabands, legitimate
Bids to make money and wealth.

Smugglers, licensed, permitted
Double the scaffold
Triple the trouble
Quadruple, the gain, the profit
Suffering the masses, the people
Yet, the Christmas fever blows hot.

## ORDERS

Orders of different kinds
Ordering from various countries
Using numerous means and channels.

The Christmas fever rolls, rocks
Orders roll in, rock out
Pressure or pleasure
Pleasure for pressure.

Orders from within and without
To  satisfy, to counter, to fortify
To sacrifice, to edify, to beautify
Orders, all around the world.

Physical, spiritual, material
Orders, in every sense of it
Cheap, costly, local, foreign
Inferior, superior, elastic, inelastic
Poor, rich, fake, real, unique, common
The Christmas orders blow hot.

Bowing, borrowing to forces
Lending hands to fate
Fate of cultured and uncultured ends.

## NEW INVENTIONS

People go to their closet
They invent whatever,
Especially if no one cares
If rules are weak
And regulations, dead
If constitutions are empty
And stipulations, scanty.

They invent good and bad
They try their hands on anything, everything
And play trial and error
People get carried away
And move with the bandwagon
As many fall victim,
Victims to the consumption.

Horrible inventions that kill
Materials, drugs, articles
A lot of businesses spring up
Just to make quick money
At the detriment of others
Because Christmas is around
Not minding the ills and harm.

## SYPHONING PEOPLE

They syphon people
Especially the ignorant ones
They deceive and fool people,
Even the learned too.

They bring out methods
Tactics, patterns, processes, types
Procedure, time, phase
In order to milk people dry.

They cook stories and news
They sell information too
True and false techniques
And people cash in
Believing it is for good.

They try, track and lurk
They go beyond normality
They fold reality and bend it
They hide clues and release dews
Dews of frustration
Netting victims like fish,
Only for Christmas and beyond.

## LOSS

As markets boom
And investments rise
People scramble over choices
Bargains and pleas catapult
Speed racers dive into businesses
Even with no feasibility and viability study.

They stumble and step on
Landing on goods and services
For and against, forward movements
In the quest for profit
As it turns loss, sometimes.

Loss and losses abound
When wrongly embarked on
Miscalculated, underestimated
Untimely ordered, mistakenly led
Loss, loss and loss
The loss that ruins lives.

The fever of Christmas
The fever that enters new year
Leaving millions sick.

## ABDUCTION OF BABIES

Babies miss, children disappear
As abductors go on rampage
And ritualists try their hands.

Abductors abduct old and young
They call for ransom sometimes
They supply to shrines too
They sell parts and organs
They kill, they dump, they fly.

Babies, innocent babies
Pregnant women, unborn babies
Women and children
Able bodied men, youths
The Christmas fever ruins some.

All manner of evil go on
Mesmerizing lives and properties
Soiling societies and foundations
Tormenting humans and humanity
The season of salvation
Bringing doom and bondage
Suffering the world at large.

## MOCKERY

Some who feel arrived
Who think they are made
Who believe they are better off
Who have questioned the Creator
Mock the poor, the less privileged.

They laugh, they scorn, they mock
They gossip, backbite, slander
They feel life is straight
Because luck favoured them.

Mockers, haters and ignorant folks
Mocking the unfortunate ones
Reminding them of their past
Remembering their miseries
Pointing their follies
And shaming them down.

The Christmas fever
It searches out evil too
It paints some ugly pictures
Trending backwardness
Slaughtering peace and tranquility.

## GOSSIP

Because people return
And are now in clusters
Stories rise and fall.

News, verified and unverified
Real, false, fake, true, harmful
Many stories to hurt
To kill, tarnish images
To hunt, haunt, and taunt.

And the timid agents help
They spread everything fast
Without sieving, thinking
Without understanding, checking
With no doubts, no chance
They fly all gossips; green.

Gossipers can be haters
They can be envious and jealous
They can be rivals and enemies
They can be friends, even
A whole lot involved,
The Christmas fever is red, crimson
Scarlet, hot, hurting, harmful sometimes.

## RUMOURS

Yes, rumours and their mongers
They satisfy themselves at will
Except they never thought.

Rumours, character assassination
Denting reputations and images
Hijacking good names and virtues
Nailing honour and respect.

Rumourmongers and evil
Circulating what they want
Feeding ears and hearts
Destroying souls and names
Planting hate and enmity
Spreading wickedness beyond.

Rumours, many a false
Winking up hands and legs
Joining heads and tails
Connecting good and bad
Mesmerizing innocence and purity
Rumours, a dew of its own
A river drowning sacredness.

## SPONSORS

Sponsors abound
They fly programs to entertain
They gradually announce their motive
Their ulterior motive, politics.

Some sponsor football matches
Some, beauty pageantry
Some, carnivals and sample forces
Making waves and names
But in the near future
You find out why.

Some hide in green grass
Though they not be green snake
But sometimes, they bite.

They promise heaven and earth
They vow to reform the earth
They tell of heavenly mysteries
As if they have been there severally
And guaranteed life everlasting.

## NEW STYLES AND FASHIONS

Fashions and styles
Pumping in, popping out
As though it would be the highest
And the best.

People do anything for it
They go the extra mile
To get whatever they want.

Craziness in the air
False living, fake dressing
Weird makeups and artificial
Limitless, outrageous boundaries.

Mad and weird fashions
Trending absurdity
Insane and wild trends
Rogues looking envogue.

Trends of inhumanity
Fashion of nakedness
Immoral and cultureless
Styles, fashions new but archaic.

## UPGRADES IN DECORATION

Decorations, here and there
Streets, roads, creeks, lanes
Shops, schools, banks, offices
Markets, malls, families
Villages, communities, states
Nations, continents, the world
Decorations, crazy colours.

Jingles, bell, pictures
Colours of Christmas
Santa Claus, father Christmas
Erections, Christmas trees
Everywhere, town, rural, urban
With whooping sums and funds.

Gigantic Christmas trees
Trees with millions of money
Contracts enriching the rich
And starving the poor
Needless, useless, mean, heartless.

Exorbitant requests and bills
Aimed at duping, raping, cheating
Outrageous Christmas decorations
Some mocking, some ridiculing.

## COLOURS EVERYWHERE

Colours everywhere
Red, gold, green, off white
In hundreds and thousands
Speaking into the air
Telling the world a story
The arrival of the saviour.

Colourful season and reason
Beautiful reason and season
Wonderful time of the year.

The media, the society, the world
Adoring, singing, praising
Stating, restating, reiterating
The essence, the impact, the importance
The uniqueness of the time.

Doubts and arguments
Loud or silent, countered or not
Everyone feels it, sees it, knows it
The saviour of the world is born
The fever of Christmas
In tune with the land.

## BALLOONS

Balloons in their numbers and colours
Sizes, types, shapes and prices
Decorations, so much with them.

Children, loving it all
Getting handful of them
Playing with them
Bursting as many as possible.

Balloons, red, green, white, purple
Blue, orange, yellow, brown
Black, indigo, Violet, cream
Long, short, small, big, tiny
Fat, zigzag, circular, triangular
Straight, curved, assorted
Adding flavour to the air
Beautifying the environment.

Some floating, some hanging
Some on the floor, ground
In rooms, parlours, corridors
Churches, parks, lounges, everywhere
Colours, wonderful, balloons.

## REALITIES

But then, realities are realities
The real side of life is real
You cannot take it away.

Realities dawn after a while
When we fool ourselves
In the name of belonging
In order to feel arrived.

Realities beckon, they stare
They ward off fantasies, then
They chase away dreams
And flood nightmares
They flaunt regrets
And preach had I known.

Realities may hide before Christmas
Only to resurface after
By then, the deed is done.

So beware of realities
They come calling after the fever,
And they can traumatize forever.

## MOMENTS

Moments, wonderful moments
Moments shared and spared
Moments reunited and ignited
Moments stolen and abused
They all, count good or bad.

Moments, quiet, or noisy
Moments, memorial or forgotten
Memorable, regrettable, or not
Affordable, durable, manageable.

Moments, golden, sparkling
Times without number
Refreshing, rejuvenating, growing.

There are moments, ungodly
Unruly, unholy, inhumane
Moments, we pray never came
Those moments that haunt.

But then, the fever rages
Calm, hot, high, low, small, big
Simple, complex, complete, complicated,
Christmas goes on.

## NEW CULTURES AND TRADITIONS

People coming home
From different areas
And numerous walks of life
Bringing back foreign cultures
And introducing strange traditions.

Newness and strangeness
Weirdness and craziness
Belongingness and knowingness
All, little or no usefulness.

Useless cultures and traditions
Needless articles and reasons
Careless lots and plots
Ignorance and foolishness
Quest for adventure
Harmful and dangerous moves.

Versatility and wideness
Coverings and coverages that mar
Fever and glamorous folly
Eagerness to die happily,
Even when death is scared to kill.

## KNOCKOUTS AND FIREWORKS

Knockouts, bangers and fireworks
Different types and sizes
Different prices and colours
With various sounds and loudness.

Some to be held
Some to be thrown out
Some to be buried half down
Some to be kindled to burn out.

Fireworks during Christmas
Fireworks on ceremonies
Fireworks at celebrations
Fireworks on the new year eve
Fireworks, fireworks on new year.

Sounds, noises, sounds, noises
Smoke, smell, smoke, smell
Thick clouds, choking soot
Beautiful colours up there
Combinations so wonderful
Harmony rays and shadows
Telling of news, news of newness
The fever is amazing and engrossing.

## JANUARY

Then comes January
In might, with might,
Strong, mean, bold, hard
Ready to pull down the weak
Eager to frustrate
Bent on hurting.

January the hardest
They call it the thirteenth month
Strange month, very raw
When realities dawn more
Mostly after Christmas fever.

January, time for change
For resolution and decisions
For revolution and reflections
When row call is personally done.

January the first month
A time to start afresh
The time to set new goals
The meanest month and season
After the mesmerizing Christmas fever.

## EMBRACING THE NEW YEAR

Then comes the new year
With its newness and freshness
Blowing up and down
As if it would reach the Everest.

Embracing the new year
Reaching out far and near
Going for growth
Spreading wings of blossoms.

The new year comes
Longing to be ushered in officially
Raiding the environment
Hooking up with people
Enlisting those interested
Enrolling those faithful
And stamping on resolutions.

Time, bit by bit
Time, then by turn
One by one, it lingers
Then fades the fever
As the year begins to dish out what it has.

## NEW RENT

And as the new year begins
Life reshuffles itself
Things quake and shake
Some fall off, some fall in
Some join, some disjoin
A whole lot takes place
Change continues its cycle.

Then, the rent expires
Time to renew or relocate
Time to increase rent
Changes of uncomfortable sorts
Triggering so many things.

New rent, new payment
Coupled with Christmas spending
As fresh as they may be,
Unnecessary expenses and expenditures backfire
Wishes, regrets, become solutions.

Those who have plans excel
Those who do not, battle more
Time may be against them
Because the fever of Christmas,
Sometimes does not spare.

## NEW HOUSE

Some pack out of their old homes
Former building or rented apartment,
And move into a new house
Especially the one they built.

Some warm and open new houses
They joyously enter in the same
And call for celebrations.

Some lay foundations sometimes
Some begin moves and ventures
That would bring more goodies.

The Christmas fever is amazing
It has good, and bad sides
People key into the one they want or feel
Depending on who they are
Where they are and how they want it.

New houses spring up
Also with the new year
Buildings, architectural uniqueness
Spelling out hard currencies
Telling of fortunes, fame and affluence
Yet questions beckon.

## SEARCHING FOR NEW JOBS

Also comes new chances
New opportunities to seek
New vacancies around,
Begging for placement
Some in the east, west
Some in the north, south
Whoever cares to relocate
Wherever one wants to redeploy,
They can try their luck.

For ones laid off by year-end
Or those who married during the season
For the ones who retired
For those who need to learn new trades
And those who gained admission
They move, they take some steps.

New entries, new applications
New choices, new places
New journeys and new life
The Christmas fever gives way
As life takes chances on us
Placing humans by gates of fate.

## LEAVING OLD BOYFRIENDS FOR NEW ONES

Even for the season
People play games
Many costly games,
Not minding the outcomes
Just for temporary pleasure.

People unfriend their friends
They disengage their lovers
And abandon their families
Because they want quick love
Fast money, raw pleasure
Lustful satisfaction.

People meet new people
And they forget old ones
The ones who have been there for them
They move on happily
Never thinking of the harm.

Unfortunately, within the short time
They are fooled properly
And the dramatic trauma lives with them.

## FAKE LIFE

The Christmas fever is fake
It catches fake people
And torments them deep.

Fake life all around
Intimidating the commoners
Forcing the ordinary man out
Compelling him to bow,
But reality sometimes forbids.

Fake life, men and women
Borrowings, camouflaging, sabotaging
Subterfuge and deceit
Lies from the pit of hell
Strangling fools who cave in
And even the wise, who slipped.

Fake life, for a limited time
Appearing rich when dead
Looking great when common
Digging self graves, self loss
Bearing heavy cross for nothing
Deceiving self in hundred folds
Because of Christmas fever.

## DESPERATION

Desperation, eagerness
Curiosity, inquisitiveness
Zeal for nonsense
Passion for useless things
Love for perishable things
Enthusiasm for lust.

Desperation to get married
Desperation to get rich,
Desperation to arrive
To wear designers
Even when hungry and baseless.

Desperation, drunk in lust
Possessed with stupidity
Troubled by anxiety
Anxiety over unnecessary things.

Desperation, leading to death sometimes
Desperation spelling foolishness
Tree of boredom and disappointment
A peg in the eyes
Covering reality and truth.

## LOOSENESS

People become loose
Looking over issues
Issues that are vital
They turn blind eyes
Jumping into whatever,
Ignoring true values.

Looseness, especially the youths
Looseness, especially the parents
Looseness, especially the society
Immorality triples in less time.

After the fever comes sickness
Disease follows up
Death may be,
In the physical realm at least.

Looseness, freedom, unnecessary ones
People go crazy miles
Doing the forbidden
Seeking the outrageous
Condoning atrocities,
Lifting the sacrilegious
And desecrating the sacred.

## CARELESSNESS

Carelessness in different parts
Old, young, men, women
Even on the roads
On highways, waterways, airways
People behave like dummies
As if they are robots, and remoted.

Carelessness over things
Things that should matter
Matters of life, that kill or keep.

Carelessness extending to children
Children harming themselves
Hooking in avoidable scenes
Scenes they know nothing about.

This carelessness has killed many
It is currently killing more
It will still kill numbers
Especially things that should not.

Nobody is perfect, none is God
Yes, humans have boundaries
But these boundaries can be manned.

## THE AIR

The air smells nice
Littering everywhere with good aroma
Airy homes, a little dusty
Whiter, harmattan, the season.

The air naturally smells
Trying to get everyone's attention
Writing a crystal message
Sending love across as well.

The Christmas fever revolves
All nooks and crannies
The world celebrates
Rejoicing in one accord.

However, troubles may arise
From faiths different and wild
Extremists who work for their god
Worshipping him in commitment.

The air, the air, the air
The cool and lovely air around
Telling tales of Christ's birth.

## THE RUSH

But the rush is weird
Everyone rushing to get whatever
Running helter-skelter,
As if nothing else matters.

The rush to belong
The rush to get fixed
The rush to dominate
The rush to look and appear sexy
Nothing matters, sex rules.

Some sellers, some buyers
Some givers, some takers
Some importers, some exporters
The world rotating along the rush.

Rush, rushers, rushing like whirlwind
Attempting to lift bans
Bans on good things
Escalating misery and penury
The Christmas fever ticks on
Climbing trees of frustration.

## AS IF IT WILL NEVER COME AGAIN

People engage in many acts
Good, bad, ugly, weird, absurd
They do so just for Christmas
As if it will never come again.

They face it squarely
Like they have been destined
Destined to do it or die.

But Christmas comes and goes
Patience catches them all,
Intertwining, interweaving, interlocking.

People play all kinds of games
Just for a couple of days
Games that endanger
Even for a lifetime.

The Christmas fever, hot and cold
Fetching lives and destinies
Disrupting links and talents,
Destroying futures and lineages.

## MISTAKES AND REGRETS

Then after awhile
Just a little while
Regrets rear their heads,
Their ugly, ungodly and stupid heads.

Regrets for costly mistakes
Regrets for messing up
Regrets for giving in
Regrets for following trends
Regrets for doing evil,
For not being real and oneself,
Big regrets for not waiting a second longer.

Regrets, mistakes, mistakes and regrets
Things that should not have been
Those that should have been,
Time, place, person, thing
Ruined in a second, in a twinkle.

The Christmas fever consumes
It is a consuming fire
Burning down, quenching
It depends on who and what
It depends on how, when, where.

## UNNECESSARY DEMANDS

Unnecessary demands
Yes, from families and friends
From colleagues, partners and teams
From workers, employers and employees
From societies and foundations
From organizations, groups
Religious, cultural, social, political branches
Targets, aims, quarters
Dates, deadlines and submissions.

Unnecessary demands and lists
Embarrassing models and modes
Maximization of time and chance
Forcing luck to be favourable
Causing fate to blink
Rush, stampede, forces that crush.

Unnecessary demands from fiancé and fiancée
From  parents, from relatives
From in-laws, staff, boss
Pulling down, pressing on goodness
Pushing away real affection
Mesmerizing duty and faith
Troubling peace and love
The Christmas fever burns deep.

## BLACK FRIDAY

Black Friday, steady
Auctions, discounts, sales
Cheap articles, excess goods
In supply, in demand
In  want, in need, in much
For buyers, for people, for Christmas.

The rush to buy in large quantity
The need to be there
The want to partake
The urge to feature
The push to sell more,
In order to make it happen.

Black Friday, Christmas fever
All over the world, beyond borders
Boundaries quaking, crashing
Loads, goods and services
Movements of people and goods
Transportation, visitation, parting
The fever is black
Blackening choices and chances
Sparing possibilities, good or bad.

## CHRIST'S BIRTH

Jesus was born
Christ was born
The advent, we expect
The commemoration of his birth.

Remember the reason
Celebrate the season
Be in line with Jesus
Be not silly nor stupid.

Stupid things mar Christmas
Silly lifestyles damp it
Do not dent Christmas
Let the fever not harm you.

Nothing last forever
Trends come and go,
Again, again, all over again
Bit by bit, turn by turn
We live and go
We experience life and death
But legacies matter,
Happy Christmas to you all.

## HAPPY CHRISTMAS

Happy Christmas to you all
Celebrate the season
Enjoy the time.

Seasons' greetings to everyone
Compliments of the seasons
Happy new year in advance
Let the newness renew us.

Happy Christmas
Happy new year
Merry Christmas
Merry new year,
Be born again
Experience a rebirth
Let the year renew you.

Resolutions, decisions, blessings
Wishes, goodness, care, love
Peace, joy, happiness, strength
All the good things of life
Many more from above
Be upon us, ours and all
Now and forever, amen.

Ngozi Olivia Osuoha

Special thanks to
Mr. Charles Onyido
(Chief Mgborogwu)

Ngozi Olivia Osuoha

Ngozi Olivia Osuoha is a Nigerian poet, writer and thinker. A graduate of Estate Management with experience in Banking and Broadcasting.

She has twenty poetry books published in Kenya, Canada, the Philippines, USA, and others. She has also co-authored one (with Kenyan literary critic Amos O. Ojwang').

She has been featured in over sixty-five international anthologies and also has published over two hundred and fifty poems and articles in over twenty countries.

Many of her poems have been translated and published into other languages, including Spanish, Russian, Romanian, Polish, Khloe, Farsi, and Arabic, among others.

She has won many awards; she is a one time *Best of the Net* nominee, has been nominated for a *Pushcart Prize*, and she has numerous words on marble.

www.ingramcontent.com/pod-product-compliance
Lightning Source LLC
Chambersburg PA
CBHW030154100526
44592CB00009B/269